Attracting
& Feeding
Wild Birds

Quick & Easy Attracting and Feeding Wild Birds

Project Team
Editor: Brian M. Scott
Copy Editor: Carl Schutt
Design: Patricia Escabi
Series Design: Mary Ann Kahn

T.F.H. Publications
President/CEO: Glen S. Axelrod
Executive Vice President: Mark E. Johnson
Publisher: Christopher T. Reggio
Production Manager: Kathy Bontz

T.F.H. Publications, Inc.
One TFH Plaza
Third and Union Avenues
Neptune City, NJ 07753

Library of Congress Cataloging-in-Publication Data
Quick & easy attracting and feeding wild birds / TFH staff.
p. cm.
Includes bibliographical references.
ISBN 0-7938-1033-7 (alk. paper)
1. Bird attracting. I. Title: Quick and easy attracting and feeding wild birds. II.
T.F.H. Publications, Inc.
QL676.5.Q43 2005
598'.072'34–dc22
2005012401

This book has been published with the intent to provide accurate and authoritative information
in regard to the subject matter within. While every precaution has been taken in preparation of
this book, the author and publisher expressly disclaim responsibility for any errors, omissions, or
adverse effects arising from the use or application of the information contained herein. The tech-
niques and suggestions are used at the reader's discretion and are not to be considered a sub-
stitute for veterinary care. If you suspect a medical problem, consult your veterinarian.

The Leader in Responsible Animal Care for over 50 years.
www.tfhpublications.com

Table
of Contents

Introduction to Wild Birds

Two of America's most popular outdoor activities are gardening and bird watching, or birding as some refer to it. What better way to observe wild birds than to attract them to your garden?

People feed wild birds for a variety of reasons. One thing is clear; many people are doing it. In fact, a previous government study indicated that one out of every four adults in the United States feeds wild birds. That's a pretty big number of people who are actively involved in this wonderfully interesting and educational outdoor hobby.

The largest attraction to wild birds is most certainly due to their often astonishing beauty. Virtually nowhere else in nature is one able to witness such a variety of colors that all seem to blend so nicely as they do with many species of wild birds. For example: Northern cardinals with their bright red plumage; American goldfinches and their color of pure sunshine; and as Thoreau so aptly put it, the bluebird that carries the sky on his back.

Other people feed birds because they are looking for a lost connection to the natural world. There is a sense of tranquility and order to knowing that no matter what is happening in our busy world, the birds are still going about their lives, as they have for millennia. A feeder filled with birds reinforces the sense that nature persists. What a wonderful way to start the day—get up in the morning, look outside, and watch the birds come to a feeder for breakfast. It really doesn't matter where you are—in a city, suburb, countryside—birds are everywhere. And birds are typically more than appreciative guests, dining wherever and whenever a repast is laid out before them.

One of the nicest things about feeding wild birds is that it's a relaxing hobby that can be done at your own comfort level of involvement. Whether you just scatter some seed on the ground or

you have a dozen or more feeders in your yard, you're feeding the birds. It's up to you to decide how involved you'd like to be (a later chapter will discuss the benefits of using feeders).

Feeding wild birds can also be a wonderful way to introduce children to the natural world. What could be more fascinating to a child than a

Attracting and feeding wild birds is a relaxing hobby that the whole family can enjoy.

brightly colored creature that flies and sings beautiful songs—and is right in their own backyard? It can lead to a lifetime of appreciation and love of nature. Feeding birds can also be a great way to teach children responsibility. Give them their own feeder and have them keep it full and clean. It will give them a connection to the birds

Children are encouraged to take on an active role with the care of wild birds. This young boy is replenishing a birdbath with new, clean water.

and nature, and fill them with a sense of accomplishment when the birds show up regularly.

Whatever your reason for feeding the birds, remember that it should be a source of enjoyment, a chance to bring the most colorful and vibrant creatures in all of nature right to your window. You will come to know your regular visitors and look forward to their arrival each day. You'll marvel as the fledglings follow their parents to your feeder and beg for a morsel of seed. Your eyes will widen as unexpected and breathtaking guests put in an appearance on fine spring days. And soon, you will learn to love it.

Once you've decided that birdfeeding is something you'd like to do, you'll need some direction on the best way to get started.

First, take a good look at your yard. Take note of the kind of trees and shrubs around your property and even in neighboring yards. Most importantly, try to identify the birds you see in your yard before the addition of any feeders. It is always a good idea to cater

Introduction to Wild Birds

Always take a good look around your yard for potential feeding and nesting sites. What looks good to you may not be so good for the birds.

to the "regular customers" rather than market a yard strictly to the "tourist trade." In other words, work on getting the birds that already call your yard home to come to the feeders you put out rather than directing your efforts toward luring migrants into your habitat.

The best place to start is with a field guide to the birds of your area. Many will tell you if the birds are likely to use feeders or not. They will also let you know if the particular species is a bird that breeds in your area or is only a seasonal resident. So, before running out and purchasing a bunch of feeders, a biological survey of your yard is in order.

Attracting & Feeding Wild Birds

Seeds: Keeping It Simple

The bags are adorned with colorful birds, a promise of color and variety the likes of which most of us who feed birds only dream of. Pictured are cedar waxwings, a handful of warblers, and a number of other birds that have never made it to the pages of any field guide. The fact is, the number of birds that actually consume seed is a small percentage of our avian population, and no amount of exotic seeds, dried fruits, or other ingredients is going to drastically change what comes to our birdfeeders.

What you should look for in your bag of birdseed, regardless of which birds are pictured on the bag, is a very simple mixture of seeds. First and foremost in any seed mixture should be black oil sunflower. You can check the ingredients listed either on a tag sewn to the bottom of the bag or printed on the back; ingredients are always listed in order of percentage in the mix. Black oil sunflower should always be the first ingredient listed, because it is the one seed most readily consumed by the birds that frequent feeders. Those with any other ingredient listed first may be designed for price, not attractiveness to the birds. Other acceptable ingredients are black stripe sunflower, white proso millet, sunflower chips or hearts, and nuts, such as peanuts, almonds, or filberts.

In some instances, white proso millet doesn't belong in a seed mix, because the birds that prefer millet prefer it on or near the ground, and certain styles of feeders discourage these birds from using them. The birds that do use the feeders sweep the millet out, putting it on the ground anyway. This isn't necessarily a bad thing, but it means that your feeders will be emptied more quickly.

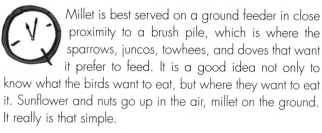

Serving Millet

Millet is best served on a ground feeder in close proximity to a brush pile, which is where the sparrows, juncos, towhees, and doves that want it prefer to feed. It is a good idea not only to know what the birds want to eat, but where they want to eat it. Sunflower and nuts go up in the air, millet on the ground. It really is that simple.

You may also want to provide peanuts in a feeder by themselves. This will give you a feeder that will be primarily for chickadees, titmice, nuthatches, and woodpeckers and one that won't be mobbed by the omnipresent house finch. There are a variety of feeders on the market today made specifically to feed peanut kernels. The smaller peanut hearts are not an ingredient you want in your mix because these seem to attract European starlings, which is considered a pest. The peanut kernel feeders actually are designed

Attracting & Feeding Wild Birds

to hold the peanut kernel so that the bird will sit there longer and eat right there, allowing you to watch them longer.

Two other seeds that are fine for feeding, but ought to be fed on their own and not in mixes are safflower and nyjer (thistle). Safflower in and of itself is not a very attractive birdseed and adds no value to a mix. However, fed by itself, safflower can be quite the problem solver. Safflower is especially unattractive to European starlings, common grackles, and even the omnipresent gray squirrel. This is especially helpful during the late spring and summer, when grackles and starlings are in the midst of their breeding season and can tend to overwhelm your feeders. Chickadees, tufted titmice, house finches, and especially northern cardinals learn to relish safflower seed. Safflower should be offered in one feeder year round to keep the birds accustomed to it. It is also a terrific seed for window feeders, keeping them for the birds many of us wish to see most.

Nyjer seed, commonly referred to as thistle, is the seed offered to attract American goldfinch; pine siskin, redpolls, and purple finch relish it as well. It too should be offered by itself in a feeder designed

This American goldfinch is enjoying a snack at a nyjer seed feeder.

Seeds: Keeping It Simple

especially for the economical dispensing of nyjer. These feeders should be placed a bit off to the side of your main feeding area, because American goldfinches prefer to feed in private and don't often fight for a seat with the more aggressive house finch at the feeder.

Sunflower seeds, nuts, millet, safflower, and nyjer can all be used in efficient ways to cover your birdseed bases. Filler seeds, such as milo, wheat, oats, canary seed, flax, and ambiguous "mixed grain products" tend to get wasted, swept off the feeder and onto the ground, where they go either uneaten or attract squirrels and mice. Although buying high-quality birdseed can certainly be more expensive at the counter, it is more cost-efficient over time. With a quality product, every single seed you offer will be eaten instead of swept out of the feeder and onto the ground, where your hard-earned birdseed dollar either sprouts or gets moldy.

Birdseed Overview

This is a quick look at what you want to find in your mixes and what you don't. The purpose of mixed birdseed should always be to increase the number of bird visits and the variety of birds visiting, not decrease cost. A good rule of thumb is not to purchase a mixed seed that is less expensive than pure black oil sunflower. This will prevent you from buying a mix in which black oil sunflower is not the primary ingredient and in which "filler" seeds have been added to fill out the bag.

Black Oil Sunflower: The single most preferred seed you can offer. It should always be the primary ingredient (listed first) in any mixed birdseed. Cardinals, grosbeaks, chickadees, titmice, nuthatches, and finches all flock to this seed. Black oil sunflower is the cornerstone of a sound feeding program.

Attracting & Feeding Wild Birds

Black Stripe Sunflower: Although eaten by some of the larger birds, such as northern cardinals and birds in the grosbeak family, it is still not as readily eaten as black oil sunflower. It is also more difficult for birds like chickadees, titmice, and nuthatches to open. In addition, it has a lower meat-to-shell ratio than oilers,  meaning that there is more shell and less meat for the birds; it is also more expensive. This seed is fine in a mix, but not as the primary ingredient.

Peanut Kernels or Splits (Halves): These are perhaps the second most attractive food you can put out for the birds. Peanut kernels, or splits, should not be confused with the tiny "peanut hearts," the little nib that is rejected in the manufacture of peanut butter. The birds that you want to attract with peanuts—jays,  woodpeckers, nuthatches, chickadees, titmice, and northern cardinals—prefer the kernels.

White Proso Millet: These small, pearly white seeds are most preferred by ground-feeding birds, which is why you don't put millet in tube feeders. The birds that can use a tube feeder will just sweep the millet out, forcing you to fill your feeder more often. Most sparrows, doves, juncos, towhees, buntings, and red-winged  blackbirds are attracted to millet. It is best served either on a platform/fly-through feeder, a slightly elevated ground feeder, or broadcast directly on the ground.

Whole Peanuts: If you want to attract jays, offer whole peanuts. Jays have been known to learn the sound of whole peanuts hitting the bottom of a feeder and will come flying in from every direction. Due to their large size, whole peanuts must be offered in open feeders; they will not pass through the dispensing system of  most hopper feeders. In addition to jays, whole peanuts will also attract crows, magpies, titmice, and woodpeckers.

Seeds: Keeping It Simple

Safflower: The problem-solver seed. What makes safflower a good addition to a feeding station is not what it attracts, but what it doesn't. Safflower is not attractive to grackles, European starlings, and squirrels. However, it loses any of that value when offered in a mix; the visitors you are trying to discourage by

using safflower will still come to the mix and either sweep away the safflower to get to the other seeds or just leave it there. This is an excellent seed to offer by itself.

Nyjer (Thistle): Nyjer is another seed for offering on its own, in a specialized feeder designed for economical dispensing of this expensive seed. It is most attractive to American goldfinches, common redpolls, and pine siskins.

Corn: Although jays and some woodpeckers will often consume corn, either cracked or whole, there are so many other things to offer these birds that they prefer even more. Corn, especially the cracked variety, is used primarily as a filler product. In warm, wet weather, cracked corn has a tendency to mold rapidly

and is not recommended. Squirrels, on the other hand, relish a good corn snack; use corn to feed your squirrels, not your birds.

Mixed-Grain Products: This is the catchall phrase that's used when a birdseed mix is designed with price in mind, not for attracting birds. It can contain wheat, oats, rice, flax, milo, canary seed, and others. Although it makes a very inexpensive seed, it also makes a very unattractive seed mix. These ingredients

are best avoided, as they contribute little to the success of your feeding station.

Species Identification

With over 700 species of birds found regularly in the United States and Canada, it should come as no surprise that dozens of species may turn up at backyard feeders. Many birds are restricted in their distribution or breed far to the north of most populated areas, appearing in the United States only during migrations and winter. A large number of birds, however, have surprisingly wide ranges in North America and can be seen in backyards from California to New York. Still other types of birds look so much alike that the casual bird watcher is unlikely to notice that there are several species involved.

The following selection is designed to familiarize you with the most common, observable birds and bird groups.

House Finch: Will visit most any style of feeder, although they have a fondness for tube-style feeders filled with black oil sunflower. They will also consume nyjer seed, sunflower chips, and safflower.

Purple Finch: About the same preferences as their more boisterous cousin, the house finch. Drawn to tube feeders filled with oilers and nyjer. They will also visit safflower sometimes.

American Goldfinch: A smaller cousin to the house finch, shares similar tastes in seeds. These beautiful finches prefer tube-style feeders to all others. Goldfinches are the main reason people feed nyjer seed. Although the American goldfinch would rather have sunflower, they seem to enjoy nyjer better than the rest of the common backyard birds.

Chickadees: Prefer small feeders that they can cling to. Demonstrate a strong preference to black oil sunflower, peanuts, and suet but may also develop a taste for safflower seeds.

Titmice: Show a strong propensity for nut feeders. Especially relish peanuts, almonds, and hazelnuts. Like their kinfolk the chickadees, titmice love feeders they can cling to.

Redpolls: Mostly attracted to tube feeders designed to dispense nyjer seed. Also fond of sunflower chips and black oil sunflower seed.

Northern Cardinal: Perennial favorite of birdfeeders in the East, they love black oil sunflower seeds, peanuts, and black striped sunflower; will develop a taste for safflower. Prefers feeders with large open landing areas; not a frequent visitor to tube feeders without feeding trays attached.

Species Identification

Grosbeaks: No other bird can go through a feeder as fast as a member of this family of seedeaters, which live up to their name. Grosbeaks (great beaks) shuck sunflower seeds faster than most people can put it out. Being relatively large birds, they prefer large hopper and fly-through feeders. They can also be attracted to large tube feeders with seed trays attached.

Doves: Mourning doves, rock doves (pigeons), and common ground doves are primarily ground feeders. They rarely open a shell, and so prefer seeds that they can swallow easily. White proso millet is the favorite of this family; black oil sunflower is also high on the list. Being fairly large, these common feeder birds prefer ground feeders, platform/fly-through feeders, and large hopper feeders.

Jays: The quintessential feeder bandits (of the avian world, anyway) will come crashing into feeders for peanuts. They seem to prefer the ones in the shell, picking up the whole peanuts one at a time, as if to check the weight to see if it's worth the effort of opening. They will also feed on peanut kernels, other nutmeats, sunflower seeds, and occasionally, suet.

Attracting & Feeding Wild Birds

Woodpeckers, Flickers, and Sapsuckers: These tree-clinging birds can all be attracted to your yard with suet. It is important to initially offer suet on the trunk of a tree so that the birds find it more easily. Downy woodpeckers can be attracted to sunflower chips, as can northern flickers. Hairy woodpeckers, red-bellied woodpeckers, downy woodpeckers, and red-headed woodpeckers can also be enticed to peanut feeders. Because most of these birds are fairly large, a good-size hopper feeder or platform/fly-through feeder best caters to them.

Nuthatches: As their name implies, nuthatches are fond of nuts and will be attracted to peanut feeders. They will also visit virtually any feeder loaded with black oil sunflower or sunflower chips. Due to their odd anatomical makeup (not being able to reach its own feet due to being a short, squat bird with very little neck), whatever a nuthatch grabs in its beak it must fly away with. It finds a crack or cranny in the bark of a nearby tree, jams the food into it, and hammers away to eat.

Sparrows, Juncos, Towhees, and Buntings: Prefer ground feeders and large open platforms to most any other design. Their food of choice is white proso millet. Indigo buntings have been known to occasionally visit a thistle feeder. Sunflower chips and peanut kernels can also be fed as an added attractant.

Species Identification

Hummingbirds: Hummers are attracted to one type of feeder, one that dispenses sugar water (nectar). What is also important to note is that you can greatly increase your chances of attracting hummingbirds by planting and/or hanging plants native to your area that would attract hummingbirds. Plants that are most effective include  trumpet vine, honeysuckle, impatiens, fuchsia, sweet William, hibiscus, butterfly bush, scarlet sage, and bee alm. Check with your local nursery for the plantings best suited to your climate.

Feeding Hummingbirds

Nectar is nothing more than a sugar and water mixture—four parts water to one part sugar—boiled and then cooled. You can make extra nectar and keep it in the refrigerator for a week or so. There is no need to add food coloring to the nectar because any hummingbird feeder worth putting up will be brightly colored enough to attract the birds. It is important to stress, however, that you must keep your nectar fresh and your feeder clean. The sugar-water solution can ferment rapidly on hot days. In fact, during extensive heat waves it might be advisable not to put your feeders out at all, as the nectar could easily go bad in just a day or so.

Feeders

Because it is nearly impossible to find one feeder that will attract and work for all the birds in your yard, a combination of three or four feeders will work best. The term used for this kind of setup is a "feeding station." The most important thing about your feeding station is to set it up where you can see it. Far too many people are overly concerned with other aspects of feeder placement, such as cover, and are then unable to view their feeders.

Feeder Placement

You need to be ready to accept the fact that you may have to "walk your birds in" to a prime viewing area. If you have never fed wild birds before, sticking your very first feeder right on the busiest window of your house will most likely not produce the results you wish to have. Start with a feeder that's within easy reach of any trees and cover, yet far enough away to exclude squirrels. As the birds get used to the feeder and recognize it as a source of food, you can slowly move it closer and closer to your chosen viewing area.

Experiment with different locations, but don't tamper with it every day. When a feeder is not performing up to expectations, the easiest and most economical variable to consider is its location. If it doesn't work, move it. But, make sure you've given your feeder ample time—two to three weeks on average—before relocating it. Always remember that this is for enjoyment. Find a favorite place to sit and work toward putting your feeders outside those windows. Kitchens and breakfast areas are always a good choice because you're able to observe the birds in the morning when they are most active, fueling up to start their day.

Types of Feeders

The next step is to think about the kinds of feeders that will round out your feeding station.

Hopper Feeders

A good way to start your backyard feeding is with a well-designed hopper feeder, basically a covered platform feeder that has a hopper, or receptacle, inside to hold seed and dispense it gradually. Many people like these feeders because they hold large amounts of seed and are attractive to a wide variety of birds. In fact, hopper feeders are second only to fly-through style platform feeders in terms of the number of different species they will attract.

There are several key features to look for in the construction of a hopper feeder. Adequate drainage is critical; the feeder should have a screen bottom or several holes drilled in the bottom to allow rainwater to drain and to facilitate the flow of air around the seed, allowing it to dry out once wet. A feeder screwed together (not

Using hopper feeders is a good way to start your backyard-feeding regimen.

nailed or stapled) will go a long way to providing you with years of trouble-free use. Feeders that are not built properly tend to fall apart quickly and don't represent a good value. Staples and nails tend to pull out, the wood is more likely to split, and your feeder is destined for a much earlier replacement than one made of at least half-inch thick cedar with zinc chromate or brass hardware. Yes, these features are initially more expensive, but they assure you of a soundly designed, long-lasting product. Also, a manufacturer that has invested time and effort into designing and producing an attractive feeder is much more likely to build it properly than one that just throws something together.

Other important elements include a good-sized roof to protect the feeding area and a large open feeding area to accommodate a large variety of birds and allow the unobstructed flow of seed. You should avoid hopper feeders with small holes that the seed is supposed to come out of. These tend to dam, leaving the birds unable to get to the seed. A hopper feeder with the aforementioned components will allow both the birds and you to benefit from years of feeding enjoyment.

Tube Feeders
The next style of feeder suited for a well-rounded feeding station is the tube feeder. A tube feeder usually consists of a plastic or Lexan

Feeders

A house sparrow is getting a quick bite to eat at a sheltered tube feeder.

tube with holes or "ports" in it and perches to allow the birds a place to land and feed. The nyjer feeder also falls into the tube feeder category, but uses unusually small ports to allow more controlled flow of nyjer. There are two advantages of using tube feeders. The first is that the tube material is almost always clear, allowing the birds (and you) to see the amount of seed inside. This also adds to the overall attractiveness of the feeder. And second, by their very nature, tube feeders are "species exclusive." What this means is that their design does not allow easy access to some birds, particularly the larger ones. Blue jays, starlings, grackles, and cardinals find the perches on tube feeders to be a bit on the small side.

Of course, this design can be both a blessing and a curse. If you are using a tube feeder as a part of a comprehensive feeding station, you may very well want to exclude the larger birds, providing an undisturbed feeding area for your finches, chickadees, titmice, and smaller woodpeckers. However, if a tube feeder is your only feeder, you may be disappointed in the absence of some of the larger and more colorful birds. But take heart, there are ways to customize your tube feeder to accommodate the larger visitors to your yard.

The simplest way to allow more diversity at this type of feeder is with the addition of a seed tray, which is nothing more than a shallow plastic dish designed to fit on the bottom of your tube. It allows cardinals, doves, jays, the larger woodpeckers, and other birds

Attracting & Feeding Wild Birds

that are uncomfortable on perches to land on the tray and feed from the lower ports. Be aware, however, that this feature may mean that your feeder is emptied more rapidly than you wish. Fortunately, due to the popularity of the design, manufacturers are making much larger tube feeders, as well as those with trays permanently built in. Tube feeders should be filled exclusively with black oil sunflower. Birds that frequent this style of feeder are only looking for sunflower and will quickly deposit millet and other seeds on the ground via bill sweeping, the process by which some birds flick seeds aside in order to find their favorite seed in a mix. Tube feeders are usually hung from tree branches, ideally well out of the reach of leaping squirrels, but more on dealing with these charming fellows later.

Platform Feeders

The most attractive feeder to many birds is the platform, or fly-through, feeder. These are open trays, either with or without a roof, that the birds have full access to. The benefits of such a design are obvious—the birds find these feeders much easier to land on, they have no problems with seed dispensing, and they come and go from whichever direction they feel most comfortable. A major advantage of the platform feeder is that there is no dispensing system to be clogged, and you are free to feed virtually any type of food you want, from sunflower seed and suet to fruit and peanuts in the shell. The disadvantage of such a design is the lack of any carrying capacity; that is, the platform feeder needs to be refilled on a more regular basis.

Feeding platforms are probably the most likely types of feeders to be visited by larger birds such as this red-bellied woodpecker.

This style of feeder is also one that requires the most drainage due to its design, especially if you choose one with an uncovered platform. Screen or mesh bottoms are essential for a feeder of this sort to perform at its best. It is also important to clean debris off this feeder regularly so as not to clog the drainage openings.

Ground Feeders

A variation on the platform/fly-through feeder is the ground feeder, which is a platform positioned low enough to the ground to attract birds that rarely leave the ground. Sparrows, juncos, towhees, and doves prefer to feed on or near the ground. These just happen also to be the birds that prefer white proso millet, which obviously makes your ground feeder a perfect place for this seed. Drainage is just as important in a ground feeder as it is in a fly-through or platform feeder. Wet, moldy birdseed is a breeding ground for germs and diseases and should be avoided at all costs. Seed that starts to smell should be discarded immediately. Ground feeders are preferable to scattering seed on the ground due to the fact that they keep the seed drier and less likely to be wasted.

Suet Feeders

Suet feeders are also a welcome addition to your feeding station. Suet, specifically, is the fat that surrounds beef kidney. Most of what is available today is the commercial variety, which has been rendered to prevent it from going rancid. These suet cakes are designed to fit into cages made for hanging suet on the trunks of trees. Beware of the "suet" that is available at most grocery stores in the meat department. What you are usually getting is the unrendered trimmings from other cuts of meat. This variety will allow the fat to spoil; it is also often combined with a low-quality seed mix to add to its attractiveness to the consumer, while doing little for the birds. Stick with the suet products packaged for birdfeeding; they are readily available and their convenience and resistance to spoiling make them worth the extra few cents.

When you initially offer suet to the birds, hang it in a suet cage or bag on the trunk of a large deciduous tree. This is where birds that eat suet make their living. Birds such as woodpeckers, titmice, chickadees, creepers, and nuthatches glean insects from the bark of these trees, excavate and/or use cavities in them for nesting, and basically spend most of their life perched on the trunk of a tree. Your odds for success in attracting birds to suet will be much higher if you present it this way. The odds of a woodpecker discovering a

Suet is usually offered to birds using a suet cage.

basket dangling in space are not very good, and it is also very difficult for the larger woodpeckers to comfortably accomplish the feat of landing on the basket. By mounting it on the trunk of a tree, you are allowing the birds to use the tree itself as the landing platform, instead of trying to balance themselves on a swinging basket.

Suet cakes are available in a myriad of flavors, and it can be fun to try the different kinds to see which your birds prefer. One word of caution, however; what is added to the suet in the way of seed (nuts, berries, peanut butter, etc.) will also make your suet attractive to squirrels. Pure suet is commercially available and is, for the most part, significantly less attractive to squirrels.

Window Feeders

Once you start attracting birds to your yard, it is only natural to want to get a closer view of your avian guests. One very easy way to accomplish this is with the addition of a window feeder to your feeding station. Window feeders are most often made of Lexan or plastic and stick to the outside of your windows via a set of good suction cups. Two concerns people have about window feeders are if the birds will come right up to the window and do the feeders really stick. Be at ease, for birds will eventually learn that the window feeder is a safe, legitimate source of food, and the feeders will stick when applied correctly. Birds are incredibly adaptive creatures, and given the proper amount of patience, will come to your window and even begin to ignore your presence. You can facilitate how quickly the birds warm up to your window feeder with several methods. One is to initially put the window feeder on a window that gets less passerby traffic than most. By doing so, you limit the number of times you scare the birds off the feeder.

The other way to get the birds to come more quickly is the application of a two-way mirror panel. Many feeders come with these built in or available as an accessory. Although they don't totally block your presence, they will mask your movement to a great degree. In regard to getting your window feeder to adhere to your window, fight your impulse to lick the suction cups to get them to stick. While this may work great at first, it will not last long. As soon as the saliva evaporates, air takes its place and your feeder comes down. A thin film of oil is generally recommended for getting suction cups to stick. Either rub the suction cups on your forehead or use a tiny amount of vegetable oil. Anything more than that will over-saturate the suction cups and cause the feeder to slide down the window.

Peanut Feeders

Peanut feeders are a relatively new addition to the world of feeders and are designed to offer whole peanut pieces (not the very fine peanut hearts) to nut-loving birds like chickadees, titmice, nuthatches, jays, and woodpeckers. The feeders themselves are made of metal screening or mesh; the birds peck at the peanut kernels and eat them right there. Many people believe that if the bird cannot immediately extract the nut, the feeder is not working properly. However, the birds that enjoy nuts do not have the ability to sit there and eat a peanut the way a finch or cardinal eats a sunflower seed. They are forced to fly away with the peanut and either hold it between their feet or wedge it into the bark of a tree to start eating it. With feeders designed so that peanuts cannot be pulled out immediately, we are able to watch birds eat that we normally would only see as a fleeting glimpse. One of the best features of a peanut feeder is that it is not usually overwhelmed by finches.

Nyjer (Thistle) Feeder

A variation on the tube feeder design is the nyjer (formerly niger) feeder. Although this feeder has often been referred to as a "thistle" feeder, the seed put through these tube feeders with tiny openings is actually nyjer,

A white-breasted nuthatch is seen here feeding from a peanut feeder.

which is imported into this country and is sterilized to prevent it from germinating. The combination of freight costs and extra labor is the reason why nyjer is often referred to as "black gold" in birdfeeding lingo.

The primary reason for adding a nyjer feeder to your feeding station is to attract goldfinches, pine siskins, and redpolls—but, most of all, American goldfinches, whose bright yellow breeding plumage is a favorite of birdfeeders during the spring and summer months. Goldfinches like nyjer more than most other birds, even though they would rather have sunflower. Because goldfinches prefer to eat alone, the best results from offering nyjer come when you place your feeder slightly outside the heavy flight zone of your feeding station. Although they will battle fiercely with one another for a seat on a feeder, they beat a hasty retreat when confronted by larger birds, especially house finches. In fact, there is even a feeder available that offers nyjer upside down, with the feeding ports located below the perches. Although American goldfinches have no problem with this feat, house finches have a very difficult time gaining any food from this feeder, thereby leaving your "black gold" for the birds you intended it for. Nyjer feeders are also, for the most part, unattractive to squirrels and can be placed in areas you would otherwise not be able to hang a feeder.

Hummingbird Feeders

An even more specialized feeder for your feeding station is one designed specifically for hummingbirds. Hummingbird feeders differ greatly from the previously mentioned feeders in that they dispense "nectar," typically in the form of a sugar-water solution. These types of feeders come in two common basic styles, the inverted bottle and the saucer. Both have their advantages and disadvantages. The inverted-bottle design allows you to put out less nectar during extremely warm spells, thereby wasting less of it (nectar spoils quickly in heat). The drawback to virtually every inverted bottle design is how difficult they are to clean. The saucer variety is becoming more and more popular due to its ease of care; however, it needs to be kept full so that hummingbirds can reach the nectar.

This introduction to feeders is well rounded but by no means all inclusive. There are thousands of feeders on the market today, some better than others. Look for longevity from a feeder, not an ultra-low price. Quality is generally not inexpensive, and a well-designed and well-built feeder will serve you for many years. Take a good look at your yard and decide which feeders will work best for you and then put them up and await your guests.

Birdhouses &
Shelters

irdhouses serve a very real purpose in a backyard habitat. However, it's important to begin any backyard birdhouse project by first making an initial evaluation of your property. Take a careful look at existing vegetation, natural shelters, food, and water sources, as well as the types of birds that frequent your area. Each species of bird has its own specific nesting requirements—some won't even use a birdhouse—so it may be important to provide a variety of houses and shelters.

In order for your efforts to be successful, four necessary environmental elements must be present. Although these aspects of a natural habitat do not necessarily need to be found within the exact limits of your property, they must be close at hand.

Basic Environmental Elements

First, a varied food source must be part of the overall plan. The nutritional requirements of wild birds will vary with different species, regions, and at different times of the year. Natural foods, commercial seed mixes, suet, fruit, insects, and nectar all become part of one major variable required for attracting wild birds. Different foods will attract different birds, and a good guide to feeding birds will give information on preferences, seasonal variations, and so forth. With some research and experimentation, you can develop the right combination of seed mixes and food choices that will compliment your bird-housing program.

Another major element is water. The source can be as simple as a faucet dripping into a shallow pan, a birdbath, or a beautifully landscaped bird pond. Depending on the size and type of the water source, other wildlife such as insects, amphibians, reptiles, and mammals will also be attracted.

The third element for attracting birds is cover. Cover, or shelter, provides protection from predators, wind, snow, sun, and rain. It becomes a place to raise young, retreat, sleep, and rest. Cover can vary in form including shrubs, brush piles, burrows, live trees, dead trees, building ledges, bridges, rock piles, and man-made birdhouses. The more cover you can offer, the more species diversity you will see develop in your backyard sanctuary.

The final element is space. All wildlife, including birds, have their own space requirement. Space requirements can vary according to the season. In general it is important to keep in mind that every pair of birds will have its own territory to defend. Each species will defend its nesting area from other members of its own kind, preventing other birds from nesting too close. The size of these territories will vary

Make sure that all the basic environmental elements are present when choosing a birdhouse site.

according to species, and for some birds these territories can be quite large.

For example, a pair of pileated woodpeckers requires nearly 100 acres of space. A pair of bluebirds may defend almost a full acre of land for nesting rights. The American robin is often seen hopelessly fighting its own reflection in a glass window or glass door, trying to drive off an unwanted intruder in its territory.

Learning as much as possible about a specific bird's range, behavior, and feeding habits will be helpful in implementing a successful home and shelter program. It's also important to remember that your efforts should not be limited to one season. The four basic needs of wildlife must be provided throughout the year if you are to continue to enjoy the birds' presence.

Now that you know how to identify the types of birds in your area as well as the necessary elements that they require, it's time to learn a little about the basics of birdhouses.

How to Make a House a Home

There are two different types of homes that can provide shelter for nesting birds in a backyard habitat. The two are generally categorized as cavity and non-cavity, based on where a bird will naturally nest. A cavity-nesting bird is one that typically nests in the cavity or hole of a dead tree or hollow tree branch; for these birds you could provide a birdhouse, also called a nest box. Non-cavity nesting birds are the birds that typically build their nest on the ledge of a building or in the fork of a tree. With these birds, you could provide an open-fronted nest box or platform for nest building.

The tufted titmouse is a common cavity-nesting species.

Homes for Cavity-Nesting Birds

Many common birds naturally nest in tree cavities and are easy to attract to a backyard and to the shelters provided there. Titmice, chickadees, nuthatches, flickers, bluebirds, swallows, purple martins, and many of the woodpeckers are just a few. However, one size does not fit all. Each species of bird should have a birdhouse built specifically for that bird. Simply put, in order to attract a specific bird to a birdhouse, certain dimensional details must be adhered to in the construction process. These specifications will suit a particular species and will prevent unwanted birds from taking up occupancy.

A number of commercially made birdhouses are usually available for purchase, often as kits or already fully assembled. They can typically be obtained from pet shops, wild bird specialty shops, feed stores, garden centers, or large retail chain stores. Keep in mind that not all manufactured birdhouses are appropriate for nesting. Many serve as wonderful ornamental additions to a garden area, but are not necessarily attractive to birds; many are not even practical for a pair to nest in. In these cases, a nice display, an empty home, and a disgruntled landlord (meaning you!) are usually the end results. Building your own birdhouse allows for a great deal of innovation and creativity, as well as control over the eventual tenants.

Do not include a perch on the outside of the house; this will discourage house sparrows and European starlings, which are considered pests by many birdwatchers and landlords, from taking occupancy. The absence of perches will also help to deter predators from taking a foothold onto the front of the house. Cavity-nesting birds do not need a perch to gain access to the inside of the house and the absence of one will help in establishing the type of bird you are interested in. However, the wood on the inside of the house below the entrance can be grooved or fitted with wire mesh to give baby birds something to grab on to when leaving the nesting box.

To help prevent predators from entering, the entrance hole should be fitted with an additional $^3/_4$-inch thick square piece of wood around the outside of the hole (drill a hole through this piece to match the hole of the nest box). The added thickness of the predator guard will help prevent the paws of cats or raccoons from being able to reach down from the outside and into the cavity of the house.

Getting Down to the Basics

A birdhouse should include some basic elements. The top of the birdhouse should be constructed to include a slightly sloping roof that extends several inches out beyond the front, providing a shaded entrance and protection from wind-driven rains. A recessed floor with drainage holes will aid in controlling the dampness, cleanliness, and ventilation of the house. Additional $^1/_4$-inch ventilation holes or slots should be located just under the roofline.

Note the slightly sloping top of this birdhouse, a feature that provides a shaded entrance to the birdhouse.

Several methods are commonly used for protecting the outside of the birdhouse from inclement weather. Cypress, redwood, and cedar woods are considered ideal materials; because of their natural weather-resistant tendencies they do not need any chemical preservatives. However, if pine and plywood are used they may be treated to sustain the longer life of the wood. The outside of the box may be sealed with a stain or with a lead-free water-based paint; another option is to apply several coats of linseed oil. Be certain that only the outside is sealed, and do not apply a sealant around the entrance hole or inside the house. Bright or ornamental colors serve no purpose for birds, which prefer light and natural colors such as grays, browns, and greens. These colors reflect heat and sunlight much better and are less conspicuous to predators. Be aware that research has shown that applying a sealant on the birdhouses will sometimes deter the use of the house for a longer time period than if no sealant was used.

The best quality birdhouses are held together with more than staples and glue. When assembling the house, use wood glue at the non-moving joints and stainless steel or galvanized wood screws to hold the pieces together. Galvanized nails may also be used, but should be used minimally and only where screws are not possible. A hinged side and/or rooftop is recommended for ease of cleaning and inspections.

A dimensional chart is formulated only as a guideline for basic construction for different species. Keep in mind that the entrance hole dimension is extremely critical. Being off by only $1/8$ inch can allow the wrong birds to gain access or prohibit the right birds from getting in. However, for most amateur woodworkers, differences in the other dimensions—if the birdhouse is slightly narrower and 2 inches taller than a given plan, for example—may not make a great deal of difference. In nature, a natural cavity in a hollow tree is never the exacting dimensions illustrated on a chart. The important point is that the house has adequate room for the parent birds and brood. Your finished product should be close to the appropriate size, sturdy, weather resistant, easily maintained, and easily inspected.

Homes for Non-cavity-nesting Birds

Open-fronted nesting boxes are designed for birds that do not nest in natural tree cavities or birdhouses but on ledges or tree branches. An open-fronted nest box, also called a nesting shelf, is most likely to be used by robins, swallows, song sparrows, and phoebes. These structures are basically a platform without a front. Some styles are also designed without sides, and sometimes without a roof, depending on the species for which it is built. The design you decide upon should be partially determined by where the shelf will be located and by how much protection it receives from the weather.

A nesting shelf is inexpensive and easy to make. It should be made of the same quality lumber and materials as a birdhouse. The only difference with these structures is that they should not be treated on the outside, but left as natural wood. For the robins, thrushes, song sparrows, and phoebes, include a sloped roof in the actual design of the platform.

A secluded and partially hidden nesting area is generally most accepted by these species. Try to position the shelf in a location that is obstructed from view with branches or vegetation of some type, such as vine arbors or shrubbery. Depending on the species of bird, 3 to 15 feet above the ground is an appropriate height. The nesting shelf table gives construction dimensions and height suggestions for specific birds.

Maintenance

For most birds, clean, empty houses are more attractive for nesting than are those containing an old nest; some birds won't even consider a box that contains nesting leftovers from the previous tenants. Once a pair of birds has raised a clutch and the birds have fledged, the box can be opened and the old nest discarded. Always be certain that the nest is truly abandoned and not newly built. If the possibility exists that the birdhouse will be used again during the same nesting season, it should simply be emptied and swept clean. Do not wash out the box with diluted solutions of bleach or other products, which can be toxic to birds.

Once the nest box or shelf is cleaned, chances are good it will become reoccupied. Many wild birds will raise two to three broods each season. Because some pairs will automatically select another site, a cleaned nest box will be ready for the next pair to move in.

After the nesting season is over, the inside should be disinfected for lice, mites, and other pests. A one percent rotenone powder or a pyrethrin-based insecticide can safely be used for this purpose. Both of these products can be applied inside the house and will quickly destroy any parasites occupying the inside cracks and corners. None of these chemicals will be harmful to birds if applied in the fall after the nesting season.

This birdhouse has a removable front—a feature that allows thorough cleaning during the off-season.

Bird shelters can be left out during the winter months or brought in out of the harsh weather. If you decide to leave them out, it is a good idea to cover the opening to keep out mice and squirrels. The white-footed deer mouse is a notorious birdhouse occupant. In addition, many squirrel species such as flying squirrels, gray squirrels, and red squirrels love to use boxes erected for screech owls, flickers, and other woodpeckers during the colder winter months. If given the chance, many squirrels will also damage and enlarge the entrance holes on nest boxes. You can either choose to let them use the box as a winter shelter and remove them in the spring or

Here is a great example of a birdhouse that has a partially hidden nesting site.

close off the hole in the fall before they attempt to set up house.

Success With Shelters

Birdhouses should be installed early in the spring or late in winter, depending on the region you live in. Most importantly, houses need to be in place before the migrating birds arrive and well before the onset of the breeding season. Many birds will establish their territories before the breeding season actually begins, so it is important to be prepared before their arrival.

Keep in mind that your yard and the surrounding properties probably all offer slightly different habitats for birds. Take note of the habitat next door as well as your own. Your neighbor's garden or shrubbery may be conducive for birds and allow for the proper placement of a birdhouse along the property line. When placing a birdhouse, it is important to remember that not all birds nest in the same area. Even the best-planned and best-made birdhouse may never be used if the proper habitat is not present for a particular bird. Some birds are not as particular as others; although not every homeowner has the habitat for

Repairs

Fall is also a good time to make structural repairs on any nest boxes, shelves, or poles. Loose nails, screws, and hinges should be repaired in late fall or early winter so you have time to get the houses back into place before the early migratory birds return.

wood ducks, woodpeckers, purple martins, or owls, most can attract a variety of songbirds, including titmice, chickadees, and robins.

Factors to consider when actually determining the site for the box should include the direction the box will face and the amount of cover it will offer the bird. A birdhouse should not face directly into prevailing winds and strong rains that could potentially enter the box and soak the interior. A partially sunny location, as opposed to dense shade, facing southeast to northeast, is ideal. However, in extremely hot regions a nest box facing directly south could easily overheat and prove detrimental to the chicks. Try to determine the location of the birdhouse before any foliage begins to fall so you can easily identify where the heavily shaded areas are.

Many birds prefer open nesting areas where they have a good view of the nest from all directions. Others will require the house to be located in an area that offers protection and privacy. Either way, there should be a clear path to the entrance hole of the house. Generally, secluded spots away from constant human activity work well. However, these secluded spots may hold other dangers. Be sure the area does not provide a hidden location for cats to sit, watch, and become potential predators of the parents as they fly to and from the nest.

Birdhouses that are attached to poles are generally more protected from predators than those that hang from branches or that attach directly to a tree trunk. Poles are considerably more difficult for predators to climb than are trees, especially if you use smooth PVC pipe to hamper any climbing tendencies. Squirrel guards or baffles, such as those that are often used for birdfeeders, will also give added protection from climbing predators when fastened to the pole under the house. Be sure to place the pole far enough away from trees or buildings that might become jumping or launching areas for cats or squirrels. Hanging the birdhouse from a chain under an eave or from a tree branch also works.

Whatever method you decide to use, be sure the house is securely attached. The weight of an adult raccoon or a gust of strong wind can easily dislodge a birdhouse that is not securely anchored and assembled. It can be quite disheartening to get up in the morning and find your bluebird house on the ground with tiny paw prints all over it. The extra effort of properly placing your birdhouses from the start will be well worth it in the long run.

How Many Birdhouses?

In lots of an acre or less, erecting more than one birdhouse for each species can be fruitless. Other than giving the bird an opportunity to choose from more than one nest, or the possibility of having another nest available after the first clutch is raised, the box will probably remain empty. Because nesting birds will defend their territory, a nesting pair is not likely to allow another pair of the same species to nest too closely. One exception is the colony-type birds such as the swallows and martins, which will nest together in large groups.

If you would like to put up several birdhouses in your yard, try to erect different birdhouses for different species of birds and keep them as far apart as possible. Generally, a distance of 25 feet works well.

A partially sunny area is usually ideal for a birdhouse location.

Checking the Birdhouse

Once a breeding pair has established residency and has begun nest-building, many people choose to make periodic inspections of the nest boxes. However, it's important that these inspections be brief and cause little or no disruption to the birds.

A hinged side wall or front wall is handy for cleaning, but actual nest inspections are best made from the top of the house. After approaching the birdhouse, lightly tap on the sides to allow the occupants to know of your presence. Slowly lift the top, make a quick visual inspection for parasites or predators, then close the top and leave the nest undisturbed. If the house has chicks in it, opening it from a hinged side or front can sometimes result in the babies hopping out. If this happens, gently pick them up and quickly put them back in the box. Don't worry about the parents rejecting them; it is a myth that birds can smell human scent on the babies and will not take them back.

One of the most important things you can do when making nest inspections is to record your findings. Nesting box records are an important way of monitoring the success of your project. By keeping records, you can determine when and where any problems such as predation began and what types of changes were successful.

Data collection can actually begin from the first observed nesting activity after the nest box is installed. When more than one house is being observed, it is a good idea to assign a number to the birdhouse and write the number somewhere on the house. Record information such as when the pair first arrived, when nest-building began, and what types of materials were included in the nest. Also record when the first egg was laid, how many eggs were laid, and when the brood hatched and fledged from the nest.

Alternative Shelters

Aside from normal style birdhouses, there are a number of alternative shelter options that you can use in certain instances. Three of the most common styles are outlined below.

Roosting Boxes

Another type of shelter you can make for birds is a roosting box. Roosting boxes are often used as a place of refuge on cold winter nights to sleep and to stay safe and warm. Even birds that do not generally use a nest box will retreat to a roosting box if the opportunity and conditions exist. Many of the larger birds such as flickers, screech owls, and kestrels prefer to sleep by themselves and will often use a nesting box throughout the year for shelter. But wrens, downy woodpeckers, titmice, chickadees, nuthatches, and many others will congregate in numbers in a roosting box on cold windy nights.

Roosting boxes should be constructed from the same quality materials as birdhouses and nesting boxes. To accommodate greater numbers of birds, roosting boxes are much larger than nesting boxes, usually about 10 inches square and as tall as 3 feet from bottom to top of roof. Because the heat from the birds' bodies will help to heat the inside of the structure, the entrance hole is made at the bottom of the box so that rising heat does not escape. The front, rather than the top, should be hinged for periodic inspections and cleaning. Stagger the perches all the

These teardrop-shaped houses are known as gourds and are popular with purple martins.

way to the top so that individual birds are not roosting on top of each other.

Place the roosting box 8 to 10 feet above the ground, facing south to take advantage of the warm sun and opposite the winter northerly winds. A naturally sheltered place away from buildings or objects that cats can jump from is also recommended. Ideally, it should be mounted on a pole with a predator guard to keep cats, raccoons, and other predators from climbing into or reaching inside the box.

Natural Shelters

Many birds benefit from our manufactured and constructed bird homes. However, much of the existing vegetation and natural terrain around us are also valuable in the entire scheme of providing shelter for our feathered friends.

A dead tree, or "snag," is looked at by many homeowners as something that needs to be cut down for firewood. However, these dead, decaying trees provide food in the form of insects and insect larvae for more than 40 species of birds and other wildlife. Snags also provide birds with a place for nesting, perching, and roosting, and a place to establish territory.

Two different types of snags are used by birds. The first, called a soft snag, is a dead tree without limbs that is in an advanced stage of decomposition. The center of the tree is soft and easily breaks apart. The second type is called a hard snag and is also a dead tree, but it has some branches and is not in a rotted or decomposed state.

Both trees can be utilized by the homeowner for backyard birds. The ideal snag is usually 6 inches in diameter and approximately 10 to 15 feet high. It is usually the case that the bigger the snag, the greater benefit it will have to wildlife. Some backyard birdwatchers will cut soft snags and mount them on their property to attract woodpeckers. Hard snags can also be useful by providing additional perches and resting places for birds. Snags make excellent additions to feeding stations and great a place for mounting suet feeders; holes can even be drilled into the side of the snag in random locations and packed with suet.

Soft snags usually have numerous woodpecker holes in them and can sometimes be made into birdhouses for chickadees, nuthatches, and titmice. Depending on the state of decomposition and where the cavities are located, the snag can be sectioned into lengths and each section can be fitted with a sloped, bark-covered roof—the result is several natural birdhouses ready for mounting. An alternative would be to mount the entire snag in an appropriate location and let the birds pick their own home. Natural tree cavities are more attractive to certain species of birds than man-made birdhouses and add a rustic touch to a backyard bird sanctuary.

Snags can also be used to mount a constructed wooden birdhouse, rather than a steel or wooden post; this arrangement is often better received by some of the more finicky birds. Regardless of how they are used, with a little creativity snags can make a very natural-looking display in a nicely planted yard.

Brush Piles

For many homeowners, brush piles are considered an eyesore, but if you have an area on your property where tree branches seem to accumulate, this pile can be an added source of cover for many birds. Brush piles are

Not Just a Pile of Branches

A simple pile of branches, however, does not always attract birds as a safe and sheltered place to retreat, nor does it qualify as a good brush pile. There is actually a right way and a wrong way to build a brush pile that will be used by many of the smaller species of songbirds as well as benefit other forms of wildlife.

Red-headed woodpeckers will often nest in man-made nests made of branches and twigs.

also used by a number of other forms of wildlife such as garter snakes, lizards, woodchucks, skunks, cottontail rabbits, opossums, and even red foxes. In addition to providing cover from inclement weather, they also provide a means of escape from predators. Several ground-dwelling species of birds such as quail, pheasant, and grouse will quickly seek refuge from predators in a thick brush pile.

Location must first be considered. Ideally, brush piles need to be situated in a sheltered area along the edges of grassy fields and woods; avoid placing them too close to your house because these piles also attract skunks and woodchucks.

Start the bottom of the brush pile with the larger and heavier materials. Heavy stumps and large rocks can be used to build a solid base and provide den sites for mammals. Continue with larger branches and limbs by crisscrossing them as you work your way up. Smaller lightweight branches should be added in the same manner, along with vines and finally evergreen branches on top. A larger limb or two can be placed at the very top to keep the whole pile from blowing apart. The finished product is usually about 5 feet in height and 10 to 15 feet in diameter. Of course, depending on the size of your yard, a smaller version can still be effective.

Many people will disassemble and burn the lighter portion of their brush pile each year before the nesting season begins. As the summer months proceed, new materials are added to begin the making of another pile for the fall and winter months.

Landscaping
for Attraction

Habitat is the single most important feature of attracting birds and other wildlife to any backyard. Simply put, habitat is a place to live that provides the basic elements of any living creature's needs: food, water, and shelter. With a minimal amount of time and effort, each of these elements can easily be provided in your own backyards by some simple landscaping adjustments.

Because birds are some of the most diverse and adaptable creatures on the planet, bird habitats can actually consist of many different things. Birds can be found in virtually any habitat on earth; they live and thrive in the subzero temperatures of the South Pole and the

Growing a variety of trees, shrubs, and other plants is the key to creating a backyard habitat that will attract multiple species.

sweltering heat of the earth's deserts. They inhabit fields and forests, mountains and valleys; some even spend all or most of their lives at sea.

Natural Beauty

The addition of native plantings, nesting boxes, and water features not only helps birds but also enhances the natural beauty of your yard. When it comes to creating a bird-friendly habitat, form must follow function. When it comes to the birds needs, the more natural the better. Be aware that by creating attractive bird habitat you will also attract other forms of wildlife. Squirrels, groundhogs, opossums, skunks, raccoons, butterflies, dragonflies, and many other creatures will find your bird-friendly habitat inviting. Welcome them as part of the well-balanced ecosystem you are creating.

Evaluating Your Habitat

The simple mix of trees and shrubs that accompanies many typical backyards caters to the needs of chickadees, titmice, nuthatches, woodpeckers, and wrens, as well as a handful of other birds. But, that's generally where the list ends. This chapter is devoted to eliminating the monoculture of backyards and to planning for biodiversity. By doing so, you greatly increase the odds of attracting many other species that call your piece of property home.

Birds and Biodiversity

It is fairly safe to say that a well-manicured suburban lawn, with maybe a few shrubs and flowers, is not going to attract a great variety of birdlife. Basically, these yards are what biologists call a "monoculture."

What this means is that the habitat is biased toward one type of grass or shrub or tree. This does not promote "biodiversity," which is one of the key concepts of a successful backyard habitat. Biodiversity means that many species are well represented, catering to the needs of a much greater variety of life. In simple English, the needs of the birds are as varied as the species of birds that populate the world, each one fitting into a niche in its

Your backyard habitat should be attractive to both you and birds.

ecosystem. The more variety you provide in your habitat—in terms of trees, shrubs, flowers, and grasses—the more diverse the variety of birds you may attract.

The Drawing Board

The first step in creating your very own backyard habitat is by taking a good look at your property and its existing features. Perhaps the easiest way to do so is to sit down with a pencil and paper and make a diagram of your yard or outdoor space; keep in mind that this can be

Landscape Redecorating

Take note of your trees (What are they, and do they serve wildlife?) and shrubs (Are they purely ornamental, or would they be better suited for bird shelter if they were relocated?). Do any of your existing plantings produce seeds, nuts, or berries? Don't overlook flowers (Do any provide nectar for hummingbirds?). What about water sources? Should you move that neglected birdbath to a more suitable location? Keep in mind any seasonal changes that occur in your backyard.

done for an urban outdoor patio, suburban backyard, or rural expanse of farmland. This will not only give you a great reference as to what's already there, but it will also show you where you have room to add.

Once you have a clear idea of what there is to work with, make a list of any elements of habitat that might be missing or in need of enhancement. Perhaps you have several birdfeeders scattered throughout the yard, but none of them seem to attract much bird action; think about grouping them together as a feeding station or moving them to a different location. Consider which types of plantings are missing and where. Remember to look at the big picture. Your habitat will be complete only after you've provided all three elements: food, water, and shelter.

As you look at your property and think about its future, keep in mind that you'll probably want a good view of what is going on outside. Plan your plantings accordingly. Put the low shrubs, vines, and ground cover nearest your window and slowly build your way up to the tallest trees. This way, as you look out your window your eyes will naturally climb up through the various life zones you've planted.

Water is a key ingredient in any bird habitat.

Attracting & Feeding Wild Birds

As always, check with your local landscape professional to see which of the bird-friendly species discussed in this book will work best for you.

Water, the Source of Life

If you can choose only one element to enhance your natural bird habitat, consider adding moving water. Although various birds are attracted to different trees, shrubs, vines, and fruit, virtually every bird is attracted to water. They all must drink and bathe all year long.

If your property already has a natural water source, you should first evaluate it for birds, not for other wildlife or its aesthetic value. The water must be slow, shallow, and reliable. If you have a lake or river on your property, this may not help you attract many prospective backyard birds. Consider adding a water feature designed specifically for the birds.

The Importance of Water

Of all the elements you can add to a backyard habitat, water is by far the one that can yield the greatest diversity of birdlife. For example, a small re-circulating pond can quickly and easily draw in a surprising variety of species. Add a mister that sprays down the leaves of nearby plants and then drips into the pond to further tempt the birds. Although it can take months, sometimes years, for habitat enhancements such as tree plantings to take hold and begin attracting birds, water may do it as soon as you walk away.

Birdbaths

The classic birdbath can be an effective way of providing water for bathing and drinking, provided that a few points are taken into consideration. First and foremost, the water must always be kept clean and fresh. Birds should not be forced to drink stagnant or dirty water. If you include a birdbath in your habitat plan, it is crucial that the water be changed daily; by doing so, maintenance should be fairly simple—unless a buildup of algae is allowed to occur. Handle algae with a stiff scrub brush and a mixture of equal parts hot water and white vinegar. If the birdbath is especially dirty, let the solution sit in the bath for an hour or two then scrub it out and rinse it well. Note that concrete baths may become stained green from algae. It may be impossible to remove all of the algae, but the bath should be fine as long as algae is not floating in the water.

Depth is another important aspect of a birdbath. Too many of those on the market today are actually too deep for birds to use. Birds such as the American robin require only between an inch and an inch and a half to bathe in; smaller birds like finches and kinglets require even less. If your birdbath is more than an inch and a half deep, try placing some flat rocks in the bath to offer varying depths, which should attract different birds. Birds are accustomed to drinking and bathing in the small trickles of water that slowly feed streams. This depth flaw is especially true of some of the more ornamental concrete birdbaths.

Although the concrete birdbath is the one that most consumers identify with, there are quite a few alternatives now on the market offering easier cleaning and more durability. The birdbath of today and beyond is either a cedar or metal frame that holds a shallow plastic bowl. The bowl is lightweight, easy to remove, and even easier to clean.

This northern cardinal is enjoying a drink at the local watering hole.

Attracting & Feeding Wild Birds

Blue jays are frequent attendees of birdbaths but will sometimes become territorial over them. In this case, provide a few birdbaths in different locations around your yard.

Just remove the bowl and bring it inside to scrub or soak overnight. The new designs have addressed other problems associated with concrete birdbaths: cracking and wearing away over time. Replacement bowls can be difficult to find, and patching is not usually foolproof, so the consumer is then faced with buying an entirely new birdbath setup. The plastic basins available for the newer wood or steel baths are easily and inexpensively replaced.

Pottery and terra-cotta birdbaths have their own advantages and disadvantages. Although pleasing to the eye, they offer little durability and can crack very easily. Their stands or pedestals also tend to be more unstable than other designs, making them less attractive to birds. Because most birds prefer a stable base for bathing, hanging birdbaths may also be avoided. Birds will occasionally visit them, but they are

No Pesticides!

It is important to note that the use of pesticides on and around any plants is to be avoided at all costs. These plants are providing food, and ingesting even the smallest amount of these chemicals can prove fatal to wildlife.

Even flowering plants should be varied. This way, a multitude of butterflies and other insects will attract a variety of bird life.

accustomed to finding water on the ground, in puddles, small slow streams, and the like. When creating a bird-friendly and natural habitat, your goal is to maximize your property's attractiveness to birds.

Many people retire their birdbaths the minute colder weather sets in each year. This is not advisable, as birds require water for drinking and bathing throughout the year. The water sources that remain available during the cold of winter are typically either moving too fast or are too deep for birds to use. For this reason, birdbath de-icers are the accepted way to make sure your birds have the ability to find water when needed, despite freezing temperatures.

Planting to Attract Birds

Part of the American culture is to have a well-manicured swath of green surrounding our homes; unfortunately, this kind of monoculture is anathema to nature. Nature is diverse; it requires many different elements to thrive. One way to achieve this diversity is to return your little patch of earth to its former, untended splendor. If you lack the patience to wait for nature to do the planting for you, there are many ways you can help things along. The most obvious of these is to plant shrubs, vines, and trees that are beneficial to birds and other wildlife. Again, a local nursery can be of great assistance. It is also important to research your climate and soil conditions to see which plantings will benefit your habitat most.

It is also becoming increasingly important that the majority, if not all, of your plantings be native plants, plants that are a normal part of your ecosystem. Although many imported or naturalized plants have great benefits for wildlife (for birds especially), these plants may take over and become invasive, crowding out less aggressive native plants. Whether it be multiflora rose or Russian olive, when birds eat the fruits from these introduced species they do not digest the seeds. As the birds fly and defecate, the undigested seeds fall to the ground and take root. Once started, many of these can take over a landscape, choking out other vegetation, thereby only favoring the birds and wildlife that benefit from that specific plant species. If you do plant any imported or naturalized plants, please take great care to keep them in check and not let them overwhelm your habitat. If you do have invasive species in your yard, remove them and replace them with native plants. The long-term benefits to you, your yard, and the wildlife that live there far outweigh any short-term losses.

Vines

AMERICAN BITTERSWEET (*AMPELOPSIS CORDATA*): Great fruit provider, but be certain you are planting the *American* Bittersweet. There are Asian species that are to be avoided due to their invasive tendencies.

HONEYSUCKLE (*LONICERA* SPP.): An excellent source of nectar and cover for small songbirds. This is yet another plant that has Asian species that you should avoid.

Large Shrubs and Small Trees

SERVICEBERRY (*AMELANCHIER CANADENSIS*): Grows between 5 and 25 feet in height and 8 to 10 feet in width. It will do best in moist, well-drained areas. It produces white flowers in the spring and is an important berry-bearing plant during the early summer. Bluebirds, robins, tanagers, and cardinals favor its berries.

Honeysuckle is an excellent plant to include in any backyard habitat.

Landscaping for Attraction

RED-OSIER DOGWOOD (CORNUS SERICEA): This is a loose, broad shrub that grows 7 to 9 feet in height and 8 to 10 feet in circumference. It will thrive in a vast majority of soil types. It produces a white berry in the late summer that cardinals, grosbeaks, waxwings, vireos, and robins and other members of the thrush family thrive on.

FLOWERING DOGWOOD (CORNUS FLORIDA): This small tree (15 to 20 feet maximum) produces a red berry that is held through fall and winter and is feasted upon by a large variety of birds, including grosbeaks, cardinals, and waxwings.

The flowers of dogwoods attract many types of insects in the spring and summer while their fruits provide food to birds during colder months.

MOUNTAIN DOGWOOD (CORNUS NUTTALLII): This hardy tree can grow to approximately 30 to 40 feet. It produces a fruit crop in clusters every fall. These berries can attract waxwings, woodpeckers, finches, and vireos.

WINTERBERRY (ILEX VERTICILLATA): This type of deciduous holly requires both male and female plants to create berries. It grows to about 10 feet in height and can be almost as wide. The red berries are held into the winter and are an invaluable food source for mockingbirds, catbirds, thrashers, bluebirds, waxwings, and robins and other thrushes.

MOUNTAIN LAUREL (KALMIA LAIFOLIA): A big, thick evergreen shrub that grows to 15 feet high and can provide a wonderful shelter for many birds and other backyard residents. It produces light pink flowers in the early summer. Deer are also quite fond of this.

NORTHERN BAYBERRY (MYRICA PENSYLVANICA): An extremely adaptable shrub that does well in virtually any soil. Its fruit is eaten by a variety of birds and is especially relished by yellow-rumped warblers and tree swallows.

The purple fruits of the arrowwood viburnum are eaten by many birds in the fall and winter months.

FRAGRANT SUMAC (RHUS AROMATICA): Growing anywhere from 3 to 6 feet in height and 5 to 10 feet in girth, the Fragrant Sumac is a shrub that can thrive in many different soils. It's also another important source of winter food for many of our backyard birds. Bluebirds,

American robins and other thrushes, as well as northern cardinals and northern mockingbirds count on this shrub's bounty to make it through rough winters.

HIGH BUSH BLUEBERRY (*VACCINUM CORYMBOSSUM*): This shrub can grow up to 12 feet in both directions and produces berries in the summer. It can attract tanagers, orioles, bluebirds, and robins and other thrushes.

Small Trees

WASHINGTON HAWTHORN (*CRATAEGUS PHAENOPYRUM*): This small thorny tree grows up to about 30 feet in height and about the same in circumference. It produces a red berry that will last well into winter. Waxwings and native sparrows are particularly fond of this fruit, and the tree's built-in armor of thorns provides excellent nest-site protection.

Red Mulberry (*Morus rubra*): When it comes to attracting birds, there are few species of plant to rival the mulberry. Its succulent fruits are devoured by orioles, cuckoos, tanagers, and many other species. It is often necessary when dealing with mulberry to make sure you have both male and female plants to produce berries. Be forewarned that birds make quite a mess with this fruit.

AMERICAN HOLLY (*ILEX OPACA*): Can grow up to 25 feet in height as well as 20 feet across. As with all holly, both male and female plants are necessary to produce berries. It bears a red berry, especially favored by thrashers and thrushes, throughout the fall and winter. Its sharply pointed leaves provide great nest security for many birds.

MOUNTAIN ASH (*SORBUS AMERICANA*): May reach heights exceeding 30 feet. It produces a orange-red berries late in the summer and holds them well into fall and early winter. These berries are readily eaten by gray catbirds, American robins, bluebirds, waxwings, and others.

Large Trees

BLACK WALNUT (*JUGLANS NIGRA*): Grows up to 75 feet, producing chemicals that are toxic to other plants, which may give it a leg up on surrounding trees, but can be a nuisance for gardeners. Check with your nurseryman or local tree specialist to see how it will fit into your ecosystem. The nuts are eaten by many species of woodpecker.

WHITE PINE (*PINUS STROBUS*): A fast-growing, very tall tree (up to 80 feet) that prefers well-drained soil. It is important to birds as a source of cover for nesting and escaping from predators. Its needles are commonly found in many bird nests, and its seeds are eaten by chickadees,

White pine is also a large-growing tree but its fine needles provide good shelter from the elements for birds—especially during the winter.

Landscaping for Attraction

titmice, nuthatches, and woodpeckers. If you do not have evergreen (coniferous) trees in your yard, this is an excellent starter tree due to its rapid growth and popularity with the birds. On any given evening many birds can be found roosting within its protective branches, either sleeping or just waiting out some inclement weather.

BLACK GUM (NYSSA SYLVATICA): This tree can reach up to 50 feet in height and prefers soil that is well drained and acidic. It provides a dark blue fruit each autumn that is readily taken by many species of bird, including American Robins, Northern Flickers, thrashers, and mockingbirds, as well as many species of woodpecker.

SYCAMORE (PLATANUS OCCIDENTALIS): A towering tree reaching heights well over 100 feet. Requires deep, moist, rich soils. The sycamore is not terribly at home in most backyards. Its hanging seed balls are consumed by house finches, purple finches, American goldfinches, and pine siskins.

CALIFORNIA LIVE OAK (QUERCUS AGRIFOLIA): A hardy species that can grow up to 75 feet tall. Produces acorns each fall. It is known to attract California quail, Steller's jays, chickadees, titmice, and many varieties of woodpeckers.

WHITE OAK (QUERCUS ALBA): Can reach 100 feet in height. The white oak is perhaps one of the most valuable trees to birdlife. Acorns are the preferred natural food for jays, nuthatches, woodpeckers, some thrushes, as well as many of the furred residents of your yard. A good crop of acorns can go a long way to ensuring a successful winter for wildlife.

Acorns are very important to the success of many animals—including birds.

Bird-friendly Flowers

What's a bird-friendly habitat without the beautiful colors provided by flowers? Many of the flowers listed below can serve double duty in your yard as well. The seeds of these plants serve to attract the birds, and the blooms can attract butterflies, the other winged marvels of your backyard habitat.

ASTERS (ASTER SPP.): Flowers attract butterflies, provide seeds for birds

BACHELOR'S BUTTONS (CENTAUREA HIRTA): Seed provider

BASKET FLOWER (CENTAUREA AMERICANA): Seed provider

BLACK-EYED SUSAN (RUDBECKIA SPP.): Seed provider, especially attractive to goldfinches

CALENDULA (CALENDULA OFFICINALIS): Seed provider

CALIFORNIA POPPY (ESCHSCHOLZIA CALIFORNICA): Seed provider

CHINA ASTER (CALLISTEPHUS CHINENSIS): Seed provider

CHRYSANTHEMUM (CHRYSANTHEMUM SPP.): Seed provider

COREOPSIS (COREOPSIS SPECIES): Seed provider, blooms attract butterflies

CORNFLOWER (CENTAUREA CYANUS): Seed provider

COSMOS (COSMOS SPP.): Seed provider

GOLDENROD (SOLIDAGO SPP.): Provides excellent cover after flower goes to seed, blooms attract butterflies

GLOBE THISTLE (ECHINOPS SPP.): Seed provider, also provides nesting material for American Goldfinch

SUNFLOWERS (HELIANTHUS ANNUUS): Provides seeds to many birds

Again, growing a variety of plants is the key to attracting many types of wild birds.

ZINNIA (ZINNIA ELEGANS): Seed provider, blooms also attract butterflies

Although this list is by no means complete, these plantings can give your yard a lot of color and beauty as well as be attractive to a great many birds. As these flowers die, let them do so on their own and leave them through the fall. They will provide food and cover during the coming winter months. As with any and all plantings, it is always best to consult a gardening professional who can properly advise as to what will thrive in your yard.

Working With Mother Nature

Lovingly neglecting your yard, or parts of it, is one of the easiest ways to enhance your bird habitat. Nature is funny that way. Leave it alone and it will do things that will amaze you. Berry-producing plants start popping up (seeds are "planted" by the birds that eat the berries). Brush piles and scrubby areas create themselves. Even sunflowers may start to grow.

In eliminating or reducing your weeding, pruning, and use of chemical controls, you must of course keep the concerns of your neighbors in mind. The back of your property along a fence or hidden corners of the yard are perhaps preferable to the front of

Landscaping for Attraction

Mother Nature's recuperative powers are awesome to behold, and within a couple years the bounty of your lack of labor will be yours for the enjoying. Give it a try and watch the results grow.

your house—at least at first. If you are fortunate enough to live on such a large piece of land that neighbors are not an issue, let Mother Nature have a good portion of your backyard. Watch it slowly but surely return to a meadow over the years. Cut a path through it so you can enjoy it, and use the area to enhance other habitat elements such as feeders and water features.

Snags and Dying Trees

Part of letting nature have its way is to let things die. Death is an integral part of nature, providing bounty for countless other living creatures, and it is the last curve in the great circle of life. Let plants that grow naturally in your yard go to seed. This will provide a supply of natural food for birds and other animals. Let trees die. As long as they pose no threat of falling on someone's home, let them die and decay naturally. There is more life going on in a dead tree than in a live one. Many birds and other creatures count on dead and dying trees for homes. One reason that humans have found a need for putting up nest boxes in our backyards is due primarily to the lack of dead and dying trees. Woodpeckers excavate their nest sites in dead trees. After they are done with them, these holes are used by secondary cavity-nesters, such as chickadees, titmice, nuthatches, great crested flycatchers, and wrens. Dead trees also attract a great many insects that provide food for the wildlife in your backyard.

If you don't have any dead or dying trees in your backyard, "plant" one. Check with a local tree service or find a downed tree yourself.

Find a good spot for it, dig a hole (at least one-third the length of the tree section itself) in the ground, stand it up, and then backfill the dirt. You can even drill some one-inch holes in the tree and fill them with suet to feed woodpeckers and other suet-loving birds. Who knows? Perhaps a woodpecker will excavate a nesting hole in it one spring.

It is worth mentioning that the absolutely worst time to start trimming, cutting, and removing vegetation from a yard is during the spring and early summer. At this time the odds of ruining a bird's nesting site increase a thousand fold. This is breeding season, a time of year of very high stress for birds.

Dust Baths

Certain species of birds, such as pheasants, quails, wild turkeys, thrashers, wrens, sparrows, and even the occasional bird of prey, have been known to wallow around in the dust. The dust gets in between their feathers, increasing their loft and thereby their ability to insulate. It also can drastically cut down on the number of parasites living on them. Birds prefer very fine dirt for their bathing, sometimes even sand. If you care to provide such a "bath" for your birds, dig a hole deep enough to accommodate approximately 6 inches of "dust." You can create your own dust mix by combining one-third sand, one-third ash, and one-third loam. Surround the area with some natural rocks or logs to keep your dust bath intact.

Birds of prey like this American kestrel appreciate a good dust bath on occasion.

Nesting Materials

You can supply birds with nesting

materials by recycling a variety of household items. Hair from your hairbrush or from your dogs or cats can be put out, as can lint from the clothes dryer. However, if you are going to provide this lint, be certain that you do not use fabric softener sheets in the dryer; these are full of chemicals that may be hazardous to birds and their nestlings. Odd pieces of string and yarn, cotton from medicine bottles, and many other things can be used as nesting material. In fact, the House Sparrow, not necessarily a bird you wish to encourage to nest in your yard, has been known to use almost anything in its nest—cigarette filters, cellophane wrappers, even yards of cassette tape.

Go Natural

Although it has been mentioned earlier, it is so important that it bears mentioning again. When tending to your enhanced habitat, please avoid the use of pesticides and other unnatural products. Many nurseries and garden centers feature products that are completely safe for birds and other wildlife. Talk to your nursery expert about how to have an attractive and safe backyard for yourself and your visitors.

Enjoy!

One of the nicest things about birdfeeding, birdwatching, and the other activities that go with them is that they can be done to suit your own level of comfort. If you want to relandscape ten acres into your own little recreation of a great eastern forest, go for it. It may take a generation or two to come around, but why not? Then again, if you are more comfortable planting one new flower for butterflies or hummingbirds each spring, that's great too. Every little bit helps, and every little bit can attract more birds into your backyard. Enjoy!